POEMS ABOUT THE GOSPEL

Patrick McCaskey

CONTENTS

Poems About the Gospel

Poems About the Gospel

Patrick McCaskey

Poems About the Gospel

*There are 150 Psalms and 150 Shakespeare Sonnets.
Here are 150 Poems about the Gospel.*

Poems About the Gospel

Christ and Evangelists

MATTHEW

The Virginal Conception of Jesus

Matthew 1:18-24

Mary and Joseph were going steady.
After a dream, they were marriage ready.
God called Joseph to be Mary's husband.
Jesus was a descendant of David.

The Holy Spirit conceived Jesus Christ.
Joseph named Jesus and took care of Him.
Joseph was an upright man who lived for
Righteousness without being self-righteous.

Mary was prepared to be God's mother.
Joseph was the guardian of Jesus.
Matthew reaffirmed the virginity
Of Mary and Jesus's divinity.

My high school prom date was a cheerleader
At Immaculate Conception High School.

The Adoration of the Three Magi

Matthew 2:1-12

After Jesus was born in Bethlehem,
Three wise men, magi, came to pay homage.
The three wise men were not the three stooges.
The three magi let the great star lead them.

They brought gifts: gold and frankincense and myrrh.
There were not white elephant or gag gifts.

From Saint Hilary of Poitiers, we know,
Jesus received gold because He is king.
He received frankincense because He is God.
Jesus was given myrrh since He is man.

The magi did not expect thank you notes.
Mary and Joseph were not registered.

Jesus Christ was full of humility.
His Father gave Him His authority.

Poems About the Gospel

The Flight into Egypt, the Massacre

Matthew 2:13-18

From the Navarre Bible commentary,
We know that, Jesus is "like Jacob who
Went to Egypt." Christ is also like
The Israeli people who left Egypt.

Jesus and Moses were saved as babies.
They were later called to save God's people.

Rachel would not be consoled for the dead.

Matthew saw the flight into Egypt and
The massacre of the Innocents as
"The fulfillment of God's plan to estab-
lish a new" covenant through Jesus Christ.

The massacre of the holy inno-
cents reminds me of abortion. I am
Pro life and so is my beloved wife.

3

Patrick McCaskey

Jesus Prepared by Fasting and Praying

Matthew 4:1-11

Before He gave the Sermon on the Mount,
Jesus Christ went into the wilderness.
He fasted forty days and forty nights.
He was hungry; the devil tempted Him.

Christ said, "Man shall not live by bread alone."
Live on every word from the mouth of God.

Jesus Christ overcame three temptations.
Jesus did not seek personal glory.
He humbly did the will of God. Amen.

When we are tempted, trust in God and pray.
Let us have fortitude and gratitude.
The grace of God leads us to victory.

The words of the Lord help us overcome
Our difficulties and our enemies.

Poems About the Gospel

Christ our Peace

Patrick McCaskey

Jesus Christ Went Fishing for Disciples

Matthew 4:18-22

From the Navarre Bible commentary,
We know that Christ called "His first disciples
To follow Him and leave everything behind."

If the Apostles had played football, they
Would have been a great team. Jesus would have
Been the coach like George Halas. Peter would
Have been the quarterback like Bill Wade.
Andrew was Peter's brother. They would have
Been used to playing catch in the yard. Let's
Put Andrew at tight end like Mike Ditka.

James and John, the sons of Zebedee, were
Known as the sons of thunder. They would have
Been the running backs like Payton and Suhey.

Christ Taught Before He Performed Miracles

Matthew 5:1-12

From the Navarre Bible commentary,
We know that "The Beatitudes proclaim
How to be fortunate, blessed." Jesus
Christ sustains hope in the midst of our trials.

The meek "do not give in to bitterness."
The merciful overlook faults and help out.
The peacemakers have inner peace and get
Themselves and others reconciled to God.

The Sermon on the Mount took fifteen min-
utes. I wasn't there, but I have typed it
And timed it because I wanted to know
How long it took for the greatest sermon.

Living the Beatitudes is as easy
As an eight-step handshake. Let's demonstrate.

Jesus Went and Told It on a Mountain

Matthew 5:1-12a

The Beatitudes begin like the Psalms.
Christ said God was constant and generous.
It's a small world; so we have to behave.
It's for us to help mend what is broken.

Even on earth, meekness is not weakness.
Jackie Vernon said, "Meek shall inherit
The earth. They'd be too scared to refuse it."

When we think about the poor in spirit,
The mourners, the meek, the righteous seeking,
The merciful, the heart clean, peacemakers,
And the persecuted, let's remember
Boy Scouts are trustworthy, loyal, helpful,
Friendly, courteous, kind, obedient,
Cheerful, thrifty, brave, clean, and reverent.

The Salt of the Earth:
The Light of the World

Matthew 5:13-16

After Christ had taught the Beatitudes,
He told the Apostles how to live them.
They were the salt of the earth, divine flavor.
They helped preserve the world from corruption.

Jesus said the Apostles were the light
Of the world for those who were in the dark.
They drew people to God by doing good
Works in a supernatural spirit.

The Sports Faith International Banquet
Is on Pentecost Vigil. We honor
High school, college, and pro athletes, coaches,
And teams for leading exemplary lives.

It's easier to be the light of the
World now because of Thomas Edison.

Patrick McCaskey

Jesus Christ Taught
the Fullness of the Law

Matthew 5:20-26

Christ wants us to be more than compliant.
You cannot be angry at your brother.
You can't utter insults at your brother.
You cannot complain about your brother.

I have seven brothers: Mike, Tim, Ned, George,
Rich, Brian, and Joseph. Jesus had none.

This passage says no thanks to resentment,
Hatred, gossip, backbiting, and slander.

The Navarre Bible notes are instructive.
Saint Augustine noted there is a
Gradation in sin and in punishment.

If my brothers have something against me,
I have to get reconciliation.
Then I'm eligible to give money.

Jesus Teaches the Fullness of the Law

Matthew 5:38-48

Jesus Christ said let someone slap you twice.
Let someone else take your coat and your cloak.
If you are forced to go one mile, go two.
Give to beggars and be willing to loan.

Jesus Christ also said pray for those who
Persecute you and love your enemies.
God makes the sun shine on good and evil.
He makes it rain on the just and the unjust.

It is easy to love those who love you.
Jesus said hello to everyone.
Keep the law to attain God's holiness.
It's a requirement, not a suggestion.

Be like our perfect heavenly Father.
The Beatitudes are my bucket list.

Patrick McCaskey

Upright Intention Throughout the Nation

Matthew 6:1-6, 16-18

From the Navarre Bible commentary,
We know that Jesus Christ "teaches that true
Devotion calls for sincerity and
A right intention, intimacy with
God without parading one's piety."

I've already given up alcohol,
Candy, desserts, sodas, and tobacco.

Many years ago, maybe last century,
Cardinal George wrote a column in the
"Catholic New World" about giving up
Resentments for Lent. It is altogether
Fitting and proper that I should do this.

For each Lent, self-denial is back in style.
If we do our best, God will do the rest.

Trusting in God's Fatherly Providence

Matthew 6:19-23

The Navarre Bible notes are instructive.
"Jesus teaches that the true treasure trove
Is made of good works done with an upright
Intention; these will obtain for us an
Eternal reward from God in heaven."

Jesus said, "Do not lay up for yourselves
Treasure on earth." Here is sound stewardship.
Save enough money for estate taxes.

Jesus Christ wisely taught that the eye is
"A lamp that provides the body with light."

Aquinas wrote, "The eye refers to mo-
tive...if your intention is sound...direct-
ed towards God...all your actions, will be
Sound, sincerely directed towards good."

Effectiveness of Prayer, the Golden Rule

Matthew 7:7-12

Jesus Christ encourages us to pray
With confidence. He knows God will listen.
If we do good unconditionally,
Then there are no limits about what we ask.

The golden rule is really cool. It is
The standard to apply. Christ is our guy.
It is in the Sermon on the Mount.
Blessings we receive are many to count.

Jesus teaches the fullness of the Law.
Love for neighbor sums up the commandments.

My father often said, "Keep the faith."
Bishop Barron says God gives us answers.
To have faith is to live outside the box.
Risk, venture, and believe the impossible.

Doing the Will of God, Building on Rock

Matthew 7:21-29

We're here to do the will of God on earth.
We're here to live the Gospel and to put
The Words of Christ into daily practice.
Then we will be doing the will of God.

Praying and fasting and going to Church
Are not enough. We must be faithful like
Job and Abraham in tribulation.

Practice the teachings of Jesus daily.
Our houses build on rock will sustain storms.
Our faith keeps us firm through trials and errors.

Jesus teaches us with authority.
May Legatus become majority.

Even God took a day off. After God
Had a day of rest, He wrote the Bible.

Patrick McCaskey

Following Jesus Christ Is Not Easy

Matthew 8:18-22

From the Navarre Bible commentary,
We know that Christ "acts with authority."

A scribe said that Jesus was a teacher.
Jesus said that He did not have a home.
A disciple saw Christ as a preacher.
The scribe could have written Him a poem.

True disciples follow Christ all the time.
"Nothing is more important than" heaven.
The Son of man had the ultimate plan.
Follow Him since He was the Son of God.

Remember an eighth-grade basketball cheer.
One, two, three, four, five, six, seven, all good
Players go to heaven. When they get there,
They repeat. Saint Mary's cannot be beat.

The Call of Matthew and Many Others

Matthew 9:9-13

Peter, Andrew, James, John were fishermen.
Matthew was a sinning tax collector.
Paul was eagerly destroying Christians.
Jesus Christ called them and many others.

The Navarre Bible notes are instructive.
"When God calls us, He does not expect us
To have great qualities; He wants us to
Listen carefully," and respond promptly.

Matthew gave up "collaboration with
The oppressive Roman regime." He took
Up cooperation with Jesus Christ.
The Apostle Matthew wrote the first Gospel.

Jesus associated with sinners.
Thank you for associating with me.

Good News: Fasting Is Not Everlasting

Matthew 9:14-15

Disciples of John and the Pharisees
Griped because the Apostles did not fast.
Jesus wanted the Apostles to eat
While He was with them. They could fast later.

Saint Augustine said fast to be humble.
Cry out in prayer. Mortify the body.
Turn your back on the pleasures of the flesh.
Hunger and thirst lead to truth and wisdom.

Johnny Carson asked fat Jackie Vernon,
"Is it true that fat people are jolly?"
Jackie Vernon was portly. He replied,
"I don't know. Why don't you ask some fat guy?"

After I fast all night, my stomach's in flight.
I break my fast with a healthy breakfast.

Jesus Raised a Girl and Cured a Woman

Matthew 9:18-26

After the daughter of a ruler had
Died, he humbled himself before Jesus.
Jesus said she was not dead but sleeping.
After the laughter, He raised her to life.

A woman had suffered for twelve years, but
She believed in Jesus. If she could touch
His garment, she would be cured. She was right.

We get to receive Communion each day.
All we have to do is humble ourselves.
Then our faith in Christ will be rewarded.
When we need healing, show faith in Jesus.

On June 13, I had surgery for
Prostate cancer. The surgery went quite
Well. I'm off the catheter and prune juice.

Patrick McCaskey

Christ is the Long-Awaited Messiah

Matthew 9:27-31

Two blind men asked Jesus Christ for a cure.
They addressed Jesus as the Son of David.
He confirmed that He was the Messiah.
But he told the blind men not to say so.

Jesus was not a great politician.
He was a humble servant for mankind.
The cured blind men were disobedient.
They spread His fame because they were joyful.

I had eye problems for quite a long time.
Then I had helpful corneal transplants.

My eyes are fine now. Here is something from
The Hebrew poet Yehuda Amic-
hai. "The passing years have calmed me and brought
Healing to my heart and rest to my eyes."

God Sent the Apostles on a Mission

Matthew 10:7-13

From the Navarre Bible commentary,
We know that "Jesus is training his twelve
Apostles for their mission, which" the Church
Continues until The Second Coming.

Jesus said that God's Kingdom had come.
That was the message of the Apostles.
Jesus Christ performed many miracles.
The Apostles went forth and did likewise.

Christ was detached from material things.
The Apostles were to imitate Christ.
Jesus game them a sense of urgency
To give up worrying about their needs.

Jesus gave the Apostles the treasure
Of peace. They gave peace when they were welcomed.

Discipleship Has Demands and Rewards

Matthew 10:37-42

Jesus before your father or mother.
Jesus before your sister or brother.
To be Jesus worthy take up His cross.
Do it always, even after a loss.

We can find Jesus through the narrow gate.
When we go to Mass, let us not be late.
If we take up the Cross, we will find life.
Let us forget ourselves, even in strife.

Our reward is heavenly reception.
We will be received without deception.
Prophets and the righteous receive rewards.
They know they are pointed heaven towards.

Let us have a cold-water cup to drink.
Disciples and children teach us to think.

Jesus Reproached His Contemporaries

Matthew 11:16-19

From the Navarre Bible commentary,
We know that Jesus Christ was accused "of
Being a glutton and a drunkard, (and)
A friend of tax collectors and sinners."

The deeds of Jesus Christ "bear clear witness
To who He is and what His mission is."

Jesus Christ made reference to a song.
The group Mercy Me had not started yet.

When Pat Paulsen ran for president, he
Countered his opponents' criticisms
Of himself with "picky, picky, picky."

The sin that I have to confess the most
Is gluttony. If I am not careful,
I may have to take up sumo wrestling.

A Parable and an Explanation

Matthew 13:1-23

Jesus left the house and sat by the sea.
When the crowds were great, He sat in a boat.
Jesus did not bore the crowd on the shore.
Public speaking for Him was not a chore.

Birds ate seeds that had fallen on the path.
Seeds on rocky ground did not have soil depth.
Seeds that fell among thorns were choked to death.
And seeds that fell on good soil brought forth gain.

The evil one snatched the seed on the path.
The seed on the rocks does not endure long.
The seed in the thorns does not yield at all.
The seed on good soil is well worth the toil.

Jesus was a master storyteller.
The parables are about God's Kingdom.

Poems About the Gospel

Stargazer

*Three Parables Show
the Way to Heaven*

Matthew 13:24-43

Seeds and weeds are grown together on Earth.
On the last day, seeds will have a rebirth.
Weeds will be burned; they are not heaven sent.
The condemned will have a permanent Lent.

A tiny mustard seeds starts out quite small.
The seed grows more than Bill Wennington tall.
A bird can settle in a tree and nest.
When the Bulls are playing, Bill does not rest.

Children grow and grow like bread from some yeast.
Let's hope they learn to take care of the least.
Our bread order was sixteen loaves a week.
As we live each day, it's fine to be meek.

Right here on Earth we have both wheat and chaff.
Let's love each other and have a good laugh.

The Miracle Food Multiplication

Matthew 14:13-21

Jesus was quite concerned about the crowd.
He cured the sick and He fed the hungry.
Jesus Christ met the needs of the people.
He was a capable and gracious host.

Jesus prefigured Holy Communion.
The Eucharist is an institution.

Jesus received great cooperation.
Israel became a well-fed nation.
The Disciples made the distribution.
Multiplication was the solution.

Christ said eternal life is a banquet.
Earthly banquets could be heaven previews.
We can do that by serving loaves and fishes.
The men volunteer to do the dishes.

Patrick McCaskey

After Jesus Prayed, He Walked on Water

Matthew 14:22-33

Jesus put the disciples in a boat.
He dismissed the crowd without being loud.
He went up a mountain for solitude.
Jesus prayed to God. He was not being rude.

The sea was rough. Jesus had the right stuff.
He showed His authority and power.
We are human so we need a shower.
Sports Faith has a good radio tower.

Peter showed his greatness and his weakness.
When we have faith, we have strength in meekness.
The Apostles' boat is like the Holy Church.
The Spirit does not leave us in the lurch.

The Beatles taught us how to twist and shout.
Our pond has snapping turtles. We stay out.

A Woman Has a Debate with Jesus

Matthew 15:21-28

A woman asked Christ to heal her daughter
Who was possessed on her way to slaughter.
At first, Christ did not answer the woman.
The Apostles asked to send her away.

Jesus said, "I was sent for the lost sheep."
The woman then asked for help again.
Jesus said, "Children's food is not for dogs."
The woman replied, "The dogs eat the scraps."

Jesus said, "O woman great is your faith."
Then He cured her daughter at that hour.
What can we learn from these humble verses?
When we ask for help, do not use curses.

All the lost sheep need help that is divine.
Jesus provides it, if we do not whine.

Papal Keys

The Chair of Saint Peter the Apostle

Matthew 16:13-19

Right after Peter had confessed his faith,
Jesus game him the keys to the Kingdom.
Pete was promised his future primacy.
He said Christ was Messiah and God's Son.

We can make this profession too, through faith.
God gave Peter and us the gift of faith.
Christ made Peter the leader of the Church.
Peter was the Apostles' quarterback.

Saints have seen Popes as Peter's successors.
Bears have also seen this Papal vision.
Peter has the Kingdom keys; we have fobs.
Those of us in Legatus have great jobs.

Legatus is Latin: ambassador.
We drive in the far-right lane for Jesus.

Patrick McCaskey

Christ Foretold His Death and Resurrection

Matthew 16:21-27

Jesus knew that He would be sacrificed.
He accepted this as His destiny.
He also knew that His death was not the end.
He would rise from death and receive glory.

Peter did not want Jesus to suffer.
Then Jesus quickly corrected Peter.
Christ had to suffer to be Messiah.
This was His mission; He accepted it.

Christ explained what commitment to Him means.
We offer ourselves as a sacrifice.
Holiness is a spiritual battle.
Mortification leads to joy and peace.

Des Plaines is the City of Destiny.
Illinois is the Land of Abe Lincoln.

Transfiguration for Every Nation

Matthew 17:1-9

We can never know The Second Coming date
But we think about it anyway
And we wonder if we're really with God now
Or just praying after some finer day

And we tell God how easy it is to be with Him
And how right His arms feel around us
But, I wrote this poem just yesterday
When I was thinking about how right this Mass might
be

And after Mass we can have more fellowship
We can win championships with sportsmanship
So we'll try and see into God's eyes right now
And just pray right here since Jesus died for our sins

The Very Purpose of Love and Marriage

Matthew 19:3-12

The Navarre Bible notes are instructive.
"Mutual self-giving of the spouses,
Together with the procreation and
Education of children calls for
Indissolubility" of marriage.

From Vatican II, we also know that
"Thus a man and a woman, who by their
Compact of conjugal love 'are no long-
er two, but one flesh' render mutual
Help and service to each other through an
Intimate union of their persons and
Their actions...the good of the children
Impose total fidelity on the
Spouses and...an unbreakable oneness..."

Jesus Christ Entered the Holy City

Matthew 21:1-11

When Jesus and the Apostles were close
To Jerusalem, He sent two of them
Ahead for an ass and a colt. This was
To fulfil what a prophet had spoken.

Christ gained victory through humility
And weakness. Jesus was a peaceful King.
He entered Jerusalem in triumph.
Garments and branches were spread on the road.

Jesus reigns because of His intellect,
His knowledge, and His great obedience.
God does not grade on a curve, but Jesus
Christ was the most universally loved man.

Family members keep a low profile.
I have the least expensive Cadillac.

A Tale of Two Sons, a Lesson for All

Matthew 21:28-32

Two sons struggled to do their father's will.
One son said no to work; then he did work.
The other said yes and then he did not.
"Blazing Saddles" Mel Brooks said, "work, work,
work."

Work is a blessing that we should not shirk.
Not only do it but do it with heart.
At the office, my father used to say,
"Work is the thing that makes our hearts sing."

The tax collectors and the prostitutes
Saw John the Baptist come in righteousness.
They believed in him and they repented.
They applied for heaven; God relented.

Appearances don't fool God Almighty.
Be authentic; work with integrity.

The Parable of the Wicked Tenants

Matthew 21:33-43, 45-46

From the Navarre Bible notes, we know that
This is about salvation history.

"Israel is compared to a vineyard."
God lavished a lot of great care on it.
Instead of good grapes, it produced wild grapes.

The tenants are like Israel's rulers.
God charged them to look after his people.
"God sent prophets...but they found no fruit."
The prophets were treated poorly or killed.

Finally, God sent His Son Jesus Christ.
The tenants are ready to kill the son.
They expect to inherit the vineyard.
They are mistaken. The vineyard went to
"A nation producing the fruits of it."

The Parable of the Marriage Feast

Matthew 22:1-14

Jesus was a master storyteller.
A king gave a wedding feast for his son.
The bride and the groom were not registered.
They did not have a rehearsal dinner.

The invited guests did not attend.
After they were invited again, they
Killed the servants who had invited them.
The king killed the killers and burned their city.

The king sent his servants to invite others.
Good people and bad people accepted.
When the king saw one who was not wearing
A wedding garment, the king removed him.

This was not the wedding of the century.
Thank God for the wedding feast at Cana.

Greatest Commandment,
Greatest Gift of All

Matthew 22:34-40

Christ teaches the two commandments of love.
Our mandate is to love God and neighbor.

The Navarre Bible notes are instructive.
Saint Bede wrote, "You cannot truly love God
If you do not love your neighbor, (nor) truly
Love your neighbor if you do not love God."

"The only true proof of our love for God:
We love and help and care for our brothers."

Saint Thomas Aquinas wrote, "when man is loved,
God is loved, because man is the image
Of God." Saint Bernard wrote, "the reason to
Love God is God; the method and means are
To love Him without methods or means." No
Other saints were quoted for this passage.

Patrick McCaskey

The Time of the Second Coming
of Christ

Matthew 24:37-44

Noah and family entered the ark.
There were two dogs, male and female, to bark.
Noah and family survived the flood.
For a long time, there was a lot of mud.

Saint Augustine said, Jesus was not sent
To give us the date of the end of time.
Saint Thomas Aquinas said, Jesus did
Not want to tell it to the Apostles.

Jesus Christ wants us to be vigilant.
Always live our lives in a Christian way.
I'll examine my conscience every day.
We will not be judged for another's sins.

Let's read both the "Tribune" and the "Sun-Times."
We cannot make lemonade out of limes.

Poems About the Gospel

Preparation for the Day of Judgment

Matthew 25:1-13

Jesus told us about the ten virgins.
Five of them were foolish and five were wise."
The foolish ones did not bring oil with them.
The wise ones brought flasks of oil for their lamps.

While they waited all of them fell asleep.
They were awakened to meet the bridegroom.
The foolish ones asked the wise ones for oil.
The wise ones sent the foolish to the store.

The foolish ones went to buy enough oil.
The wise ones and the bridegroom went inside.
By the time the foolish ones were prepared,
It was too late. The foolish were locked out.

Like mature Boy Scouts, let us be prepared.
My father said, "Be alert at all times."

Patrick McCaskey

**Christ Arose and Appeared
to the Women**

Matthew 28:8-15

Jesus first appeared to holy women
Because they had been faithful and valiant.
Then Jesus appeared to the Apostles.
He had not seen them since the Last Supper.

Matthew avoids giving minor details.
The Resurrection was magnificent.
It was extraordinary.
Easter Sunday is a Hall of Fame day.

The soldiers who were stationed at the Tomb
Were given bribes to say that the body
Of Jesus had been stolen. Matthew wrote
In glorious, humble disagreement.

Soldiers of Christ do not take bribes, but we're
Allowed to accept Confirmation gifts.

42

Herald of the Messiah

MARK

Isaiah the Prophet, John the Baptist

Mark 1:1-8

Isaiah the prophet was a writer
Who was smart enough to let God use him.
He was an Old Testament advance man.
He told us all about John the Baptist.
John was the New Testament advance man.
He told us to repent for forgiveness.

John the Baptist was not a real fun guy.
He was not mellow; he could sure bellow.
He called everyone a brood of vipers.
He would have sent Boy Scouts looking for snipes.
Instead of loaves and fishes, he ate locusts.
He was not a listener; we listen.

We hear him say, "Jesus is mightier."
Let's be grateful for Isaiah and John.

Christ Was Tempted Before His Ministry

Mark 1:12-15

After Jesus was baptized, he fasted.
He did not have any cake or ice cream.
The Spirit drove Jesus to the desert,
Before the Raiders moved to Las Vegas.

The temptation shows the humanity
Of Jesus. He did not yield to Satan.
The angels ministered to Jesus Christ.
He did not lord his greatness over them.

If we want God's Kingdom, we must repent.
Every day is Christmas; each day is Lent.
Repentance and belief saved the good thief.
Reconciliation leads to salvation.

After Satan provided temptation,
Jesus gave us Gospel proclamation.

Patrick McCaskey

The Leprosy Left Him,
He Was Made Clean

Mark 1:40-45

From the Navarre Bible commentary,
We know that "In the gestures and words of
This leper seeking a cure from Jesus,
We can see his prayer (which is full of faith),
And his delight once he is cured...Jesus'
Own gestures and words show his compassion..."

After I had graduated from high school,
The Pat McCaskey Award was started.
It went to the member of the track team,
Who had the most acne on his back.

Many years ago, cancer, basil cell
Carcinoma, was removed from my back.
It wasn't the curing of a leper,
But it was a helpful cure for cancer.

Four Friends Help a Paralyzed Man Get Cured

Mark 2:1-12

Jesus came to town; the news spread quickly.
Quite soon there was a large crowd around Him.
Four clever friends made a hole in the roof.
They were men of faith, not vigilantes.

They lowered their friend, a paralyzed man,
On a stretcher, through the hole in the roof.
Jesus forgave the paralyzed man's sins.
Then the man was no longer paralyzed.

Max Swiatek is number one on the Bears'
Longevity list: sixty-seven years.
His wife, Irene, shaved him while he slept so
He could get right to work in the morning.
When someone returned to work after sur-
gery, he asked, "How was your vacation?"

Jesus Did the Right Thing on the Sabbath

Mark 3:1-6

After Jesus had entered the temple,
He saw a man with quite a withered hand.
The denigrators and the second guessers
Were hoping Jesus would make a mistake.

Christ talked to the man and asked a question.
The silence of the Pharisees was not consent.
After Jesus had cured the withered hand,
The Pharisees worked hard on the Sabbath.

At the Mass we honored Saint Anthony.
Tony lived by himself in the desert,
Since he did not know about Walden Pond.
He prayed and fasted except on Sundays.

Like Jesus and Saint Anthony, let us
Always strive and thrive to do the right thing.

Jesus Christ Appointed the Twelve Apostles

Mark 3:13-19

Jesus Christ showed great initiative.
He called twelve men. They responded promptly.
The Apostles were called for special roles.
They were appointed to be with Jesus.

Then the Apostles were sent out to preach.
God the Father had sent His Son Jesus.
Then Jesus sent His chosen Apostles:
Two-man delegations for all nations.

The Apostles called sinners to repent.
That is why the Apostles had been sent.
They cured the ones sick in body and soul.
To fulfil the will of God was the goal.

The Apostles were excellent teammates.
They were secure in Christ and not afraid.

Patrick McCaskey

Do Not Sin Against the Holy Spirit

Mark 3:22-30

The scribes said Christ acted with the devil.
Jesus had an eloquent rebuttal.
He said their accusation made no sense.

Jesus provoked a conflict with Satan.
Christ won. He did not work against Himself.
Jesus was more powerful than Satan.

Jesus forgave sinners and ate with them.
Closeminded people were not forgiven.

If we sin against the Holy Spirit,
We're like those who reject doctors and cures.
Let us appreciate and be open
To the graces of the Holy Spirit.

Thank God for Lincoln's House Divided Speech.
He was an eloquent unifier.

Parables of the Lamp and the Measure

Mark 4:21-25

The teaching of Jesus Christ is a light
For the whole world. The light should be passed on.

The Kingdom of God can penetrate hearts.
The light of Jesus is extremely strong.
At the end of time, the Second Coming,
Everything will be visible to all.

Jesus is talking to the future of
The Church. He wants them to listen to Him.

The grace of God is a treasure. Every
One of us will be held accountable.
If we respond to grace, we will get more.
If we don't respond, we will be made poor.

Let's also listen to Saint Augustine.
"If you say, enough, you're already dead."

Patrick McCaskey

The Seed and the Mustard
Seed Parables

Mark 4:26-34

From the Navarre Bible commentary,
We know that "The parables of the seed
And the mustard seed...are based on the
Idea of growth; that of the seed speaks of
The Kingdom's...gradual development;
That of the mustard seed..." tremendous growth.

I had to plant corn. The garden in the
North side yard was eighty feet by six feet.
It had to be roto tilled, horse manured,
Roto-tilled again, and then raked smoothly.

Two eighty-foot rows two feet apart down
The length or thirty-nine rows two feet a-
Part across the width? I decided to go
With two eighty-foot rows down the length.

From the Demoniac into the Swine

Mark 5:1-20

There was a man with an unclean spirit.
He lived like an animal in the tombs.
He was unclean without humanity.
Satan had the man. Then the man saw Christ.

Jesus was much stronger than the devil.
Christ exorcised the demon into swine.
The swine herd numbered about two thousand.
Satan led them to be drowned in the sea.

So the man recovered his dignity.
He wanted to go and follow Jesus.
Jesus wanted the man to stay right there.
The man was to talk about God's mercy.

We can stay where we have been planted. We
Can give witness to God's mercy right here.

Patrick McCaskey

Light on the Rotunda

The Martyrdom of Saint John the Baptist

Mark 6:14-29

The Navarre Bible notes are instructive.
Saint John the Baptist was the Precursor.
He prepared the way of the Messiah.
People regarded John as a prophet.
They travelled great distances to see him.

"Herod had a certain respect for John
And liked to hear him speak, and yet ended
Up beheading him." The birthday feast was
Wild. The young woman's dance was seductive.
The king made a terrible oath. These are
Examples of how not to behave. Lust
Led King Herod into a great sin.

Jim Finks said of my dancing, "It looks like
You would rather be taking a beating."

Jesus Christ Elicits Admiration

Mark 6:53-56

Christ and the Apostles took a boat ride.
When they got to Gennesaret, they moored.
The Gennesarenes recognized Jesus.
They brought sick people on pallets for cure.

Jesus went to villages and cities.
The sick were brought to the market places.
They asked to touch the fringe of His garment.
All of those who touched the fringe were made well.

Jesus elicited admiration.
The crowd was grateful for the miracles.

Bishop Barron has written about sports.
"Think of heaven as a kind of game,
Involving many participants gathered
Together around a common purpose..."

Jesus Christ Stresses Purity of Heart

Mark 7:1-8, 14-15, 21-23

From the "Workbook for Lectors" we know that
"Jesus prefers to associate with
An amiable, if somewhat unti-
dy, group rather than...critics with clean hands."

Jesus declared that all food is clean.
Sin begins in the interior life.
Jesus healed with just one look of true love.
Bing Crosby sang "True Love" to Grace Kelly.

God restores our heart with a tender gaze.
We can do the same the rest of our days.
Husbands can give their wives the look of love.
Parents can look at their children with love.

Jesus Christ looks at us with compassion,
Even if we do not like poetry.

Jesus Cured a Man Who Was Deaf and Dumb

Mark 7:31-37

The Navarre Bible notes are instructive.
Jesus worked a miracle to show "the
Saving power of his human nature."
Christ opens our ears to hear His Father.
We get salvation through the sacraments.

According to Mark, Jesus told people
To be silent about three miracles:
The curing of a man with leprosy,
The raising of a little girl from death,
And the curing of a deaf and dumb man.

"Jesus wanted people to come to His
Mission...in light of His death on the cross."

The people were like Edith Bunker. They
Could not stifle themselves or dummy up.

Jesus Makes the Deaf Hear and the Mute Speak

Mark 7:31-37

From the Navarre Bible commentary,
We know that Christ "now works a miracle
Using gestures that symbolize the
Saving power of his human nature."

Jesus opens our ears to enable
Us "to hear and accept the word of God."
Christ told the people to be quiet about
The miracle, but they did not listen.

Last year, I had surgery to remove
Non-cancerous growth from my inner ear.
It was an opportunity to do
John Byner's impersonation of John
Wayne as a brain surgeon. John Byner said,
"We're gonna have to yank it outta there."

Jesus Christ Foretells His Resurrection

Mark 8:34-9:1

Jesus Christ taught us about salvation.
We get it through suffering and the cross.
Let us take the pledge: not our will but God's.
Then we will get the blessing of heaven.

God is even more wonderful than the
World that He created in just six days.
We should love God more than we love the world.

Heaven will be better than cars and homes.
Holy angels will be great cheerleaders.
We'll be back in the Garden of Eden.

Before an Easter Mass, I said to the
Celebrant, "There's a big crowd out there. I
Guess they heard that I was the lector." The
Priest responded, "You solved the mystery."

The Curing of an Epileptic Boy

Mark 9:14-29

When Jesus and Peter and James and John
Came down from a high mountain, they came to
The other disciples and a great crowd.
When the crowd saw Jesus, they were amazed.

The father of an epileptic boy
Asked Christ to stop the seizures of his son.
The disciples were not able to help.
Christ invites the father to pray with faith.

Then Christ taught the disciples in private.
After His ascension, they had to pray.
Through the curing of an epileptic,
Christ teaches us to pray with confidence.

Mark Twain said, "I have the calm, quiet con-
fidence of a Christian, with four aces."

Patrick McCaskey

Jesus Wants Us to Avoid Scandal

Mark 9:41-50

Jesus said accept water in my name.
Do not cause little ones to be ashamed.
If one of your hands causes you to sin,
You should cut it off and be more thin.

Just avoiding sin is not quite enough.
The occasions of sin are not good stuff.
More earthly goods are not our destiny.
Let's have souls ready for eternity.

From the Navarre Bible commentary,
We know that Isaiah 66:24
Is Mark 9:48, "where their worm does not
Die, and the fire is not quenched," that is hell.

"Anything that might lead us to commit
Sin must be cut short..." Enjoy your dinner.

Indissolubility of Marriage

Mark 10:2-16

From the beginning, we're male and female.
A lineup like that does not become stale.
Saint John Paul II said married couples are
Called to "total mutual self-giving."

From the lectors' workbook, we know that "life-
Long monogamous marriage is the ideal."
Here's a slight "Young Frankenstein" rewrite, "Fi-
delity, no escaping that for me."

From the Navarre Bible commentary,
We know that "the Kingdom of heaven be-
longs to those who receive it like a child."
We don't merit it. We accept God's gift.

Let's believe like children, love like children,
Abandon like children, pray like children.

Patrick McCaskey

A Rich Young Man Says No to Poverty

Mark 10:17-27

Christ called a rich young man to follow Him.
Unlike the first disciples, he said no.
Material things can become false gods.
When we know and love God, we can say yes.

It's important to keep a low profile.
I have the least expensive Cadillac.

My goal is to keep the Bears in the fam-
ily until The Second Coming. In
The meantime, I shall continue to tithe.

When I started working for the Bears, my
Hair was brown, curly, and thick. Now my hair
Is white, straight, and thin. God is protecting
My marriage. I was too good looking

The Sons of Zebedee Make a Request

Mark 10:35-45

James and John were the sons of Zebedee.
They were well known as the sons of thunder.
They would have been like Payton and Suhey.

Christ asked, "Are you able to drink the cup?"
They wanted to be at the right and left
Of Jesus. Instead, Jesus had two thieves.

The Passion of Jesus was baptism.
His sufferings purified the whole world.

Christ said, "I am here to serve not be served."
Let us go out therefore and do likewise.

Let us see who can be the most humble.
Let us not be proud of humility.

When I started working for the Bears, I
Was everyone's assistant. I still am.

The Healing of the Blind Bartimaeus

Mark 10:46-52

Bartimaeus was a blind beggar. He
Was very determined and insistent.
When Christ called him, he threw off his mantle.
He showed his faith when he talked with Jesus.

Jesus asked Bartimaeus, "What do you
Want me to do for you?" Bartimaeus
Replied, "My teacher, let me see again."
Bartimaeus became a disciple.

Commentaries in the Navarre Bible
And Word on Fire Bible are instructive.
Saint Josemaria Escriva and
Bishop Bob Barron are Hall of Famers.

I used to have to watch television
With binoculars. My sight is restored.

The Parable of the Wicked Tenants

Mark 12:1-12

Jesus Christ was a great storyteller.
From the Navarre Bible commentary,
We know that "In this parable Jesus
Provides a summary of salvation
History and of his own life and work."

God wants His chosen people to be good.
There have been times when we were reluctant.
The servants are symbols of the prophets.
The son who was killed represents Jesus.

Like Old Testament Joseph who was not
Bitter to his brothers who had sold him,
Jesus tells this story without rancor.
It is all part of God's wonderful plan.

Jesus Christ started the excellent Church.
Through the Spirit, we're not left in the lurch.

Patrick McCaskey

The Greatest Commandment of All from Christ

Mark 12:28-34

The scribe asked a well-intentioned question.
Jesus devoted time to teaching him.
The scribe understood the reply of Christ.
After the reply, there were no more questions,
Not even from Detective Columbo.

Saint Augustine said: love God is the first
Commandment; love neighbor is the first ac-
tion. If you love your neighbor, you can see God.
If you love your neighbor, your eye is cleansed
To see God. John said, "If you do not love
Your neighbor whom you see, how will you be
Able to love God whom you do not see?"

Name three Chicago first-round draft choices
With the first name Kyle: Long, Fuller, Schwarber.

Jesus Censures the Scribes: The Widow's Mite

Mark 12:38-44

From the Navarre Bible commentary,
We know that "Jesus denounces any
Disordered desire for human honours."

When Bishop Sheen accepted an award,
He thanked his writers: Matthew, Mark, Luke, John.
We also have Bishop Barron, Archbishop
Chaput, Anthony Esolen, Scott Hahn.

From the "Workbook for Lectors," we know that
The widow has the "right intention and
Generous spirit. As she gives the lit-
tle which is her all, she becomes the mod-
el of one who entrusts herself to God."

A mite is a small coin formerly current.
We can give even when it is not Lent.

Patrick McCaskey

A Poem from a Former Patrol Boy

Mark 13:33-37

Jesus said that we should be vigilant.
From "Navarre" we know we must be vibrant.
This is a parable; let's be prepared.
It is not good for us to know the time,
Since we would only be good at the end.
Being faithful is our mountain to climb.

Jesus is the traveling householder.
Peter is the vigilant gatekeeper.
We're the servants who are here to wash feet.
Getting to heaven would be really neat.
Our job is to obey the Commandments
In the Spirit of the Beatitudes.

We are the sentinels and the sentries.
Like patrol boys, let us be attentive.

Jesus Gave the Apostles a Mission

Mark 16:15-18

From the Navarre Bible commentary,
We know that "Jesus summarizes the
Apostles' mission...to preach salvation
To the whole world..." baptize everyone.

Let the record show, I have been baptized.
Father Bird presided at Saint Mary's.
George Stanley Halas was my godfather.
Flossie McCaskey was my godmother.

Like the Apostles, I have a mission.
I am a lector: I am a speaker.
My themes are Chicago Bears' history,
Faith based education, and sports and faith.

Football has Commandments and Beatitudes
And if the Apostles had played football.

Patrick McCaskey

LUKE

Annunciation and Incarnation

Luke 1:26-38

Nazareth was not mentioned in the Old
Testament. But that is where the angel
Gabriel announced to Mary that she
Would be the mother of Jesus, God's Son.

The Son of God would become human with-
Out diminishing His divine nature.
Joseph and Mary were going steady.
The announcement helped Mary get ready.

The Old Testament is truly fulfilled.
Jesus Christ will have the throne of David.
Christ "will reign over the house of Jacob."
The Kingdom of Jesus will have no end.

Eve ate an apple; Mary was humble.
Eve disbelieved; Mary conceived Jesus.

72

Mary, the Immaculate Conception

Luke 1:26-38

Gabriel wrote a prayer, the Hail Mary.
Nazareth was City of Destiny.
Joseph & Mary were obedient.
Then Gabriel said, "Do not be afraid."

Jesus descended from a king, David.
The Kingdom of Jesus will have no end.
Since Jesus was God's Son, He was holy.
Since Mary was God's Mom, she was holy.

Mary and Elizabeth were remarkable.
Gabriel was gone, like the Lone Ranger
Who rode off into the sunset before
We could thank him. "High ho Silver away."

Rodgers and Hammerstein's Cinderella sang,
"Impossible things are happening every day."

Patrick McCaskey

Visitation

Mary Went to Visit Elizabeth

Luke 1:39-45

Abraham was the father of nations
Because he believed what God had told him.
Mary became the mother of God be-
cause she accepted the challenge on faith.

God gave Mary intense preparation.
The angel gave Mary revelation.
Mary traveled far for visitation.
Her Son became all our incarnation.

Mary's cousin Elizabeth was pregnant.
Elizabeth's son, John, leapt in her womb.
What Elizabeth said became a prayer.
We have "The Hail Mary" because of her.

From Saint Ambrose, we know "both women be-
gan to prophesy, inspired by their sons."

The Visitation: The Magnificat

Luke 1:39-56

Here is the Second Joyful Mystery.
Mary traveled to see Elizabeth
Who lived with her husband Zechariah.
She was quite pregnant with John the Baptist.

Elizabeth's words praised God and Mary.
Jesus would love even the contrary.
Mary would thank God for all He had done.
God the Father would even send His Son.

God shows mercy to each generation.
The Hail Mary is a great sensation.
Mary and her cousin had a visit.
Then Mary returned home, since she missed it.

The Magnificat was Mary's Praise Song.
At the All School Mass, let's all sing along.

The Shepherds Found the Holy Family

Luke 2:16-21

The shepherds were nearby Israelites.
They went in haste to nearby Bethlehem.
They opened their hearts and received great joy.

Let us be grateful to the Apostles.
They replaced circumcision with Baptism.
Long before we are in an earthly tomb,
Now we can name babies in the womb.

When we are tempted to complain about
Accommodations, let us remember
A stable was good enough for Jesus.

If we ever have one more flight delay,
We can still thank God for the Wright brothers.
If the Bears ever lose another game,
We can still be grateful for our mothers.

Mary, Jesus, Simeon, and Anna

Luke 2:22-40

Mary underwent purification.
Joseph & Mary made an offering.
Jesus was presented in the temple.

The Holy Spirit led Simeon.
He said that Jesus was the Messiah.
Jesus is salvation for all mankind.

Mary shares in the sacrifice of Christ.
Anna wanted Israel's redemption.
Simeon and Anna were messengers.
The Holy Spirit worked through them and us.

As a child, Jesus learned to do His chores.
Jesus Christ is full of wisdom and grace.

Even as adults, we have to do chores.
We must have domestic tranquility.

The Finding of Jesus in the Temple

Luke 2:41-52

Jesus Christ was full of wisdom and grace.
Jesus referred to God as His Father.

From the "Catechism of the Catho-
lic Church," we know that "The finding of Je-
sus in the temple is the only e-
vent that breaks the silence of the Gospels
About the hidden years of Jesus" Christ.

When I was a student at Saint Mary's
School in Des Plaines, City of Destiny,
We put J.M.J. at the top of our
Papers for Jesus, Mary, and Joseph.

Call letters for Catholic Radio
In Hartford, CT are WJMJ.

Let us listen to God's word and live it.

John the Baptist Preached in the Wilderness

Luke 3:10-18

From the Navarre Bible commentary,
We know "John is the last of the prophets."

Because the Messiah will soon be here,
We should get ready and do penance for
Our sins, mend our ways, and "be able to
Receive the grace that the Messiah brings."

Ancestry does not secure salvation.
We get salvation through true repentance.

John the Baptist was very transparent.
If you have two cloaks, give one to the poor.
Just collect a just amount of taxes.
Don't extort, falsely accuse, or complain.

The message was preached in the wilderness.
God's grace brought it to the best-selling book.

Jesus Makes Us Acceptable to God

Luke 4:21-30

The Garden of Eden was heavenly.
Jesus Christ will help us get to heaven.

Christ lived in Nazareth for thirty years.
Jesus was an indigenous leader.
He does not need a doctor; He's the cure.
Instead of envious, let's be grateful.

We receive God's love through the sacraments.
Jesus wants us humble and confident.
He will purify and sanctify us.

The people of Nazareth were fickle.
Jesus did not passively accept their
Fury. He went away to pray alone.

No poet is accepted in his own
Parish, except of course Seamus Heaney.

Jesus Christ Went Fishing for Disciples

Luke 5:1-11

When Peter, James, and John fished on their own,
Without Jesus, they were unsuccessful.
With Christ as their guide, the fish did not hide.
They jumped into the boat; they did not float.

My favorite sandwich is tuna on rye,
Without the contamination of celery.

From the Navarre Bible commentary,
Here is what I learned from the passage.
Remember the past with gratitude; live
The present with enthusiasm; look
Forward to the future with confidence.

"Like all those chosen by God for a mission,"
Jesus said to Peter, "Do not be afraid."

Poems About the Gospel

Enlightened

Pray with Humility and Confidence

Luke 5:12-16

From the Navarre Bible commentary,
We know that "The man's disease made him very
(very) ugly, and people shunned him for fear
Of contagion. Sin has the same effects."

We sin. We need forgiveness and God's grace.
"With humility and confidence, we
Will often borrow the leper's words and
Pray, 'Lord if you will, you can make me clean.'"

And "the Gospel shows us Jesus going
Off alone, to pray. We too need to set a-
Side time for frequent, personal prayer in
The midst of our daily activities."

Now let's review. If we ask Jesus to
Cure our ugliness, He will make us clean.

Jesus Has a Discussion on Fasting

Luke 5:33-39

The Navarre Bible notes are instructive.
Jesus fasted before He ministered.

Penitential fasting is important.
During ministry Christ ate joyfully.
The teaching of Christ "calls for new wineskins—
Deeper repentance, profound renewal."

Receiving teaching with a sincere heart,
Helps us prevent the sport of backsliding.

Saint Leo the Great emphasized three things.
It is important to abstain from food.
The soul should give up iniquity
And the tongue should cease to bear false witness.

Let's smile when self-denial is in style.
Thank God fasting is not everlasting.

Jesus Prayerfully Chose the Twelve Apostles

Luke 6:12-16

Before important events, Jesus prayed.
He prayed before He chose the Apostles.
He extended His work through the Church which
Was to last until the end of the world.

Perry Como sang "Til the End of Time."
My goal is to keep the Bears in the
Family until The Second Coming.

The choosing of the twelve was the first draft.
Later, the first National Football League
Player draft was in 1936.
Joe Stydahar was the Bears' first draftee.

As the two-thousand-year old man Mel Brooks
Said, "Jesus and His twelve friends came into
My store, but they didn't buy anything."

Poems About the Gospel

Luke Has Four Beatitudes and Four Woes

Luke 6:17, 20-26

The Navarre Bible notes are instructive.
Saint Luke recorded that Jesus Christ preached
In open spaces to show how "open
Our Lord was to all people and how his
Message was directed to everyone."

Those without iPad can read God's Word.
Those who are hungry don't have to eat kale.
Those who weep can still hear Jim Gaffigan.
Those Christians who are scorned are like prophets.

Those who are rich are already consoled.
Those who are quite full may need to downsize.
Those who are laughing might soon be crying.
Those who receive praise may soon get a raise.
While they're alive, they're required to tithe.

The Teachings about Love of Enemies

Luke 6:27-38

Jesus said, "love your enemies, do good
To those who hate you, bless those who curse you."

The Navarre Bible notes are instructive.
"Divine mercy is the forgiveness of sins."

Bishop Bob Barron said, "When you turn the
Other cheek hold your ground." The second slap
Will be less powerful; it's a back hand.

George Halas and Vince Lombardi had great
Respect for each other. I never won
Against Art Contreras of Maryville.
I wanted my parents to adopt him.

Alan Swanson of Stony Brook and I
Tied for first in a fall cross-country race.
Together, we finished ahead of Choate.

A Parable about Integrity

Luke 6:39-42

If you have a log in your eye, you are
Not the guy to remove another's speck.

Credibility needs integrity.
Purity is an opportunity.
Salvation is a possibility.

George Bernard Shaw said, "All great truths begin
As blasphemy." And Young Frankenstein said,
"Destiny, no escaping that for me."

The Navarre Bible notes are instructive.
Saint Theophilus of Antioch, loved
By God, said, "Show me that the eyes of your
Mind see and that the ears of your heart hear."

After a conflict resolution, Chip
Hilton's heart sang with a great confidence.

The Holy Women Provide for Jesus

Luke 8:1-3

Jesus preached the good news of salvation.
The twelve Apostles were Hall of Famers.
Christ helped many women become holy.
They gave Him devotion and assistance.
There was cooperation with Jesus.

Mary Magdalene was the first witness
To the Resurrection. Joanna was
Also witness to the Resurrection.
Susanna was also helpful to Christ.

Saint Monica prayed for Saint Augustine.

Saint John Paul II interpreted Scripture.
Men are adequate because of women.

My mother, Virginia; my wife, Gretchen;
And my daughters-in-law provide for me.

Jesus Gave the Apostles a Mission

Luke 9:1-6

Christ called a meeting of His disciples.
He gave them power and authority.
Jesus told the Apostles how to live.
They were to travel light like Pope Francis.

Churches started where the Apostles went.
They were blessed because they were heaven sent.
A delegation for every nation
Cooperation is a sensation.

Holy Church has a specific mission.
Love everybody without condition.
Come to fruition without sedition.
Tom Hanks was in "The Road to Perdition."

Let's have confidence in God's providence.
There's no limit to God's benevolence.

Saint Paul

Herod is Curious about Jesus

Luke 9:7-9

From the book "Who's Who in the Bible," we
Know that Herod "had John the Baptist im-
prisoned and...ordered John's execution."
John had criticized Herod for marry-
ing the wife of Philip his half-brother.

From the Navarre Bible commentary,
We know that "Jesus' doings provoke the
Key question: 'Who is He?' The Gospel points
Out that the people were unsure as to
The answer and that Herod was perplexed."

Saint John Paul II wrote, "Only the faith pro-
Claimed by Peter, and with him by the Church
In every age, truly goes to the heart
And touches the depth of the mystery."

Peter's Faith and the Passion Announcement

Luke 9:18-22

Jesus prayed. Then He asked the disciples,
"Who do the people say that I am?" The
Disciples answered John the Baptist or
Elijah or one of the old prophets.

Christ asked, "But who do you say that I am?"
Peter professed his faith that Christ was God.
Christ said the disciples should tell no one.
He was not eager to be crucified.

From the Navarre Bible notes we know that
Saint John Vianney wrote, "a person who
Loves pleasure, who seeks comfort, who flies from
Anything that might spell suffering, who
Is over-anxious, who complains, who blames
...a person like that is" not living right.

The Consummate Need for Self-Denial

Luke 9:22-25

Transfiguration then Resurrection.
Communion is Transubstantiation.
Jesus told us to take up the cross daily.
To help us we can go to daily Mass.

Follow Jesus through Saint John Vianney.
Don't love pleasure. Don't seek comfort. Don't fly
From anything that might spell suffering.
Don't be overanxious. Do not complain.
Do not blame and become impatient.

Amen, I say to you, my Aunt Julie
Used to say, "What does it profit a man
To gain the world and lose his Aunt Julie?"
Her husband, my Uncle Bob used to say,
"I'm all alone at the foot of the cross."

The Transfiguration of Jesus Christ

Luke 9:28b-36

After Peter confessed his faith in Christ,
Jesus took Peter, John, and James to pray
On the top of a mountain. Then Jesus
Was transfigured into quite dazzling white.
Peter's confession of faith was confirmed.

Jesus revealed that the way of the cross
Would lead to his entry into glory.

The Navarre Bible notes on this passage
Lead to Catechism 555 and
Saint Thomas Aquinas. "The whole Trinity
Appeared: The Father in a voice; the Son
In the man; (the) Spirit in the shining cloud."

"Christ's Passion is the will of the Father."
Jesus Christ died and rose as God's Servant.

Seventy Disciples Have a Mission

Luke 10:1-19

Jesus Christ sent seventy disciples,
Two by two, to places where He would preach.
They were chosen to be the advance men.
They were taught to say, "Peace be to this house."

The Navarre Bible notes are instructive.
"Our Lord...requires of them detachment and
Abandonment to divine providence."

"The actions and words of the disciples
Are, like those of Jesus, a call from God
To repentance, which must come from the heart."

Saint Josemaria Escriva wrote,
"Don't doubt it: your vocation is the greatest
Grace our Lord could have given you. Thank Him
For it." I thank God for my vocation.

Patrick McCaskey

The Seventy Return, Jesus Gives Thanks

Luke 10:17-24

The disciples were thrilled to be a part
Of Christ's mission since they saw its power.
Jesus asked them to look deeper. The real
Celebration was God had chosen them.

Jesus expressed His joy because humble
People understood Him and accepted
The word of God. It was like this school all
Class reunion. Everyone was helpful.

Jesus declared that He knew God the Father.
Christ had a dual role. He revealed God.
He was God. He played defense and offense.
God made Himself accessible to us.

The school bore us without being boring.
The priests and nuns gave us our destiny.

The Kingdom of God Overruled Satan

Luke 11:14-23

Critics said Jesus worked with the devil.
Christ denied the charge and warned the critics.
They saw people had been freed from Satan.
Their stubbornness gave him a place to work.

This passage is blunt and polemical.
The devil is strong; he enslaved mankind.
Christ is stronger; He defeated Satan.
We need to make room for God's Kingdom.

The Navarre Bible notes are instructive.
Saint Caesarius of Arles said that,
"At our baptism, we were made into
Temples of the Holy Spirit." Don't sin.

When we are at home, when we are away,
The Holy Spirit helps us every day.

The Unclean Spirit and Seven Others

Luke 11:25-26

The house of the unclean spirit was swept
And put in order. So he recruited
Seven other unclean spirits who were
More evil than he. They lived together.
Snow White and the seven dwarfs were better.

From the Navarre Bible notes, we know that,
Saint Caesarius of Arles said that,
"Since Christ at his coming cast the devil
Out of our hearts to make his temple and
Dwelling-place there, we should do everything
In our power, with the help of his grace,
To ensure that" we don't dishonor Christ.

The unclean spirit had seven others.
Jesus had twelve Apostles and the Church.

Responding to the Word of Jesus Christ

Luke 11:27-28

From the Navarre Bible commentary,
We know that "The Tradition of the Church
Has always read these words as great praise for
The Blessed Virgin." She believed God's word.

From the Catechism of the Catho-
lic Church," 149, we know that "Throughout
Her life and until her last ordeal when
Jesus her son died on the cross, Mary's
Faith never wavered. She never ceased to
Believe in the fulfillment of God's word.
And so the Church venerates in Mary
The purest realization of faith."

Mary was not the least bit contrary.
She helped everyone, even the most wary.

Jonah and Saint Teresa of Avila

Luke 11:29-32

From the Navarre Bible commentary,
We know that "The Ninevites did penance
Because they acknowledge the prophet
Jonah and accepted his message.
Jesus is greater than Jonah…Christ's life
And preaching are a call to conversion."

From the Magnificat, we know that
Saint Teresa of Avila advised,
"Let nothing disturb you, let nothing
Frighten you, all things are passing away:
God never changes. Patience obtains all
Things. Whoever has God lacks nothing; God
Alone suffices." This is holy advice.

My sister Anne's middle name is Terese.

Poems About the Gospel

Jesus Came to Establish Division

Luke 12:49-53

Our division is the NFC North.
We often play Lions, Packers, Vikings.
When you turn the other cheek, stand your ground.
Let's establish a solid running game.

Some attend every game; some do not.
Let there be amnesty for the no shows.

Jesus did not come to establish peace.
That's why football is a collision sport.
Some root for the Cubs; some root for the Sox.
The important thing is we're all Bear fans.

Jesus was here to divide households.
Thank God for homilies to explain why.
We must follow the voice of Jesus Christ
From conception to a natural death.

Patrick McCaskey

Interpretation of the Present Time

Luke 12:54-59

Talk about weather is superficial.
Salvation talk is supernatural.

Christ gave us miracles, His life, and His
Teachings to show He is the Messiah.

Now is the time for our correct conduct.
Get ready for judgment; don't be condemned.
The Trinity is the most Supreme Court.
Their decision is the ultimate one.
On Judgment Day, we either pass or fail.

Hardened hearts lead to incorrect judgments.
With Christ, we can live with humility.

Here is a quote from writer James Thurber.
"Let us not look back in anger or for-
ward in fear, but around in awareness."

Jesus Cures a Woman on the Sabbath

Luke 13:10-17

From the Navarre Bible commentary,
We know that "By performing this cure on
A sabbath, Jesus shows his divine mag-
nanimity...the sabbath is a day
For praise of God and a day of joy. That
Is why it made sense to cure the woman...?"

Jesus Christ had mercy and tenderness.
Persistent compassion imitates God.
Let us stand up straight and glorify God.
If you cannot stand up straight, do your best.

On the day of rest, we are God's guest.
It does not have to be on a Sunday.
Monday through Friday, I ride ten miles each
Day on a stationary bike. On most
Saturdays, I run four hundred meters.

Patrick McCaskey

Obtain Salvation Through the Narrow Door

Luke 13:22-30

The Navarre Bible notes are instructive.
From Vatican II, we know that we should
Use the strength of Christ's gift to follow
In His footsteps; conform to His image;
And do the will of God in everything;
Devote ourselves to the glory of God
And to the service of every neighbor.

"God will judge us...on our response to grace."
Christ said eternal life is a banquet.
Let all banquets be previews of heaven.

Let there be Caesar salad and skim milk,
And loaves and fishes. I'll do the dishes.
I am the loader; I have a system.
I am trying to be the most humble.

Parables: The Lost Sheep and The Lost Coin

Luke 15:1-10

God Almighty desires everybody:
Incarnation for civilization.

The shepherd found the lost sheep and rejoiced.
The woman found the lost coin and rejoiced.
The shepherd and the woman are like God.
When a sinner repents, there is much joy.

From the Navarre Bible commentary,
We know that "In the face of our weakness,
God does not stand idly by: he goes out
In search of what is lost and makes every
Effort to find it...But, above all, he
Rejoices—as he does when we seek him."

Christ received sinners and ate with them. Thank
You for receiving and eating with me.

Patrick McCaskey

The Parable of the Prodigal Son

Luke 15:11-32

The younger son offended his father.
Both of them need reconciliation.
There is forgiveness and a fatted calf.
The older son is selfish and jealous.
He also needs reconciliation.

The Navarre Bible notes are instructive.
"Meditation on this passage will help
Us to be optimistic (and) confident."

In relation to the parable of
The prodigal son, I've been the younger
Son. I have been rebellious. I have been
The older son. I have been resentful.

Now my goal is to be the father. For-
Give others as I have been forgiven.

Poems About the Gospel

The Parable of the Unjust Steward

Luke 16:1-13

Parables helped Jesus convey teachings.
He taught the Apostles to be clever.

Saint Josemaria Escriva wrote,
"What zeal people put into their earthly
Affairs...When you and I put the same zeal
Into the affairs of our souls, we will
Have a living and working faith. And there
Will be no obstacle that we cannot
Overcome in our apostolic works.

The Navarre Bible notes are instructive.
"at all times, in little things and big things,
In wealth or poverty our focus should
Be on God." Christ said "And I tell you,"
God alone is the source of every good.

Saint Margaret of Scotland

Feast Day of Saint Margaret of Scotland

Luke 17:20-25

Jesus said the Kingdom of God is here.
It was not observed; it was not announced.
Jesus told His disciples to stay put.
"Do not go off, do not run in pursuit."

Jesus said He had to suffer greatly.
Then He would be like lightning in the sky.
His generation would soon reject Him.
On Easter He would triumph by and by.

Saint Margaret of Scotland was saintly.
She founded monasteries and churches.
She diligently took care of the poor.
She brought travelers to Saint Andrew's shrine.

Andrew was an original Apostle.
He saw Jesus as lightning in the sky.

The Revelation about God's Kingdom

Luke 17:26-27

Jesus reminded His disciples about
The days of Noah and the days of Lot.
The ark saved Noah and his family.
Fire and brimstone destroyed Sodom. Jesus
Encouraged the disciples to obey.

Here is David Steinberg's routine about
Lot and his wife. As they were leaving Sod-
om and Gomorrah, the twin cities, Lot's
Wife said, "Lot, what's the matter with you? That
Was fun back there. How come you always do
What God tells you to do?" Lot responded,
"Dear, God told me to tell you to look back."

Dick Smothers asked his brother Tommy, "If
Someone told you to jump off a bridge, would
You do it?" Tommy replied, "Not again."

Jesus Told the Unjust Judge Parable

Luke 18:1-8

The Navarre Bible notes are instructive.
"The parable of the unjust judge is
A very eloquent lesson about the
Effectiveness of" prayer perseverance.

Our mandate is to pray without ceasing.
Let us overcome laziness and pray.
If we are a praying delegation,
Then we will be a great sensation.

In the public square, we can say a prayer.
During a quiet walk, let us not squawk.
At your work station, pray for our nation.
As we do a task, don't forget to ask.

"Prayer nourishes faith, but faith, in turn, grows
When it is enlivened by prayer." Amen.

Jesus Christ Wept Over Jerusalem

Luke 19:41-44

The Navarre Bible notes are instructive.
"When the procession reaches a place that
Looks out on a good view of the city,"
The disciples were surprised when Jesus wept.

Christ worked many signs in Jerusalem.
The Covenant will be sealed on the cross.

Jesus visits each of us. He teaches
Us through the preachings of the Holy Church.

"He grants us forgiveness and grace through the
Sacraments. If we are faithful and at-
tentive to his word, we can ensure that
Our Lord has not come in vain." So be it.

The Bears have never played in Jerusalem.
That sounds like a prayer request. So be it.

Jesus Drove the Robbers from the Temple

Luke 19:45-48

From the Navarre Bible commentary,
We know that the "cleansing of the temple
Is a reminder of the respect due
To the House of the Lord. Christian temples
That house the Blessed Eucharist are
Worthy of even greater reverence."

Halas Hall is a place of work and not
A den of thieves. It is a halfway house
To heaven. Instead of saying, "Please be
Quiet," we say, "Please become a mime."

Thank you for listening. This is better
Than talking to myself. It is great to
Be with you. Have a Hall of Fame day.

Jesus Christ Said We Will Rise from the Dead

Luke 20:27-38

The Sadducees did not believe in the
Resurrection of the body. Whereas,
The Pharisees did accept that doctrine
In Scripture and in oral tradition.

The Sadducees asked Christ a sly question.
Jesus Christ talked about the general
Resurrection. There will be no need for
Marriage. We will have happiness and peace.

Mark Twain said, "There's no humor in heaven."
James Thurber and E. B. White wrote a book
With the title "Is Sex Necessary?"
In the afterlife, we will not need it.

We won't need rehearsal dinners because
Christ said eternal life is a banquet.

Patient Endurance in Every Trial

Luke 21:5-19

Fasting, solitude, silence, and singing
Of psalms are helpful in saving your soul.
Add thanksgiving, prayer, and humility,
Firmness and strength through patient endurance.

Even if you win every game, you won't
Play every down. When you are off the field,
You can help others by being a clown.
Provide some respectful comic relief.
Help other people work through their grief.

Capital improvements like fixing the
Parking lot and the track were not like
Detention and being stretched on a rack.

Our bodies are temples of the Holy
Spirit. I need to downsize my body.

Patrick McCaskey

Tribulation and the Second Coming

Luke 21:20-28

Armies circle cities and people flee.
Nations in distress will be quite a mess.
Christ's victory is a great sign for me.
Bear trials patiently; get eternity.

While we work on sod, we endure for God.
Do good works with patience and persevere.
If we give up halfway along the path,
Then we will get what we deserve: God's wrath.

The Navarre Bible notes are instructive.
From Saint Cyprian, let us remember,
"he would lose the fruit of what he had done
...he did not finish what he had begun."

Jesus will be with us on Earth again.
He will be here for both women and men.

The Fig Tree Shows Us the Kingdom of God

Luke 21:29-33

Jesus Christ told a fig tree parable.
When trees come out in leaf, summer is near.
He also said that God's Kingdom is near.
First, the Apostles had to rake the leaves.

From the Navarre Bible notes, we know that
All that Jesus "has said will come to pass."

Figs on trees create a heavenly breeze.
When you eat Fig Newtons, think of heaven.

Alan Lerner wrote "I Talk to the Trees."
It's from the musical "Paint Your Wagon."
Tommy Smothers thought that it was goofy.
"Oh, hello stage. You used to be a tree."

At a roast, what did Foster Brooks say to
Billy Graham? "I really like your crackers."

Patrick McCaskey

Jesus Christ Had a Hall of Fame Thursday

Luke 22:14-23:56

On Holy Thursday, Christ instituted
The Eucharist, foretold the treachery
Of Judas and the denial of Peter,
Appealed to the Apostles, prayed and
Agonized in the garden, arrested.

The Apostles became priests who offered
Communion when they celebrated Mass.
The Apostles shared in the trials of Christ.
They also shared in the triumph of Christ.

The Bishops are Legates of Jesus Christ.
They are leaders as foot-washers for God.
The devil was successful with Judas.
Jesus prayed for Peter who was later
Restored. Peter gave his life for the Lord.

The Episode of the Good Repentant Thief

Luke 23:35-43

The good thief repented. He also said
Jesus didn't do anything wrong; Jesus
Was innocent. The good thief said that he
Believed in Jesus. Christ gave him heaven.

Saint Augustine gave up dissipation.
Then he became a Doctor of the Church.
Confession of crimes leads to punishment.
Confession to God leads to salvation.

From John Paul II, we know that forgiveness
Is more powerful than sin. Forgiveness
Leads to reconciliation to God
And in relationships between people.

I used to be in high school detention.
Now I'm on my high school governance board.

Patrick McCaskey

Walking, Talking to Emmaus

Luke 24:13-35

They were walking to Emmaus,
Seven miles from Jerusalem.
Then Jesus walked and talked with them,
But they did not recognize Him.

They walked and talked; they walked and talked.
Jesus was a great listener.
They talked about Christ crucified.
Women could not find His body.

After Jesus had heard them out,
He told them Christ had to suffer.
Then He would enter His glory.
So said Moses and the prophets.

Christ stayed with them in Emmaus.
He broke bread; then He disappeared.

Jesus Christ Appeared in the Upper Room

Luke 24:35-48

Jesus Christ showed that He was flesh and bones.
He was not just a guy named Smith or Jones.

Jesus was very hungry because He
Had not eaten since Holy Thursday night.
After He had asked for something to eat,
The Apostles gave Him something quite light.

"They gave Him a piece of baked fish." It was
A secular communion. When they served
Loaves and fishes, there were a few dishes.
Then there was time for Jesus in His prime.

They did not have dessert even though it
Was the end of the original Lent.

The Apostles went to every nation.
They brought the humble news of salvation.

Patrick McCaskey

JOHN

John the Baptist Leads Us to Jesus Christ

John 1:6-8, 19-28

God sent John to give us testimony.
John's testimony was not a phony.
The Baptist did not say he was the one.
He told us about Christ Who was God's Son.

The questions for John were very many.
None of them were worth even a penny.
John was patient and did not obfuscate.
He was very clear, unlike Watergate.

John was not Christ, Elijah, or prophet.
He did not sell equipment for Moffett.
Isaiah had told us John would be here.
Repent for our sins and be of good cheer.

John was not worthy to untie sandals.
And yet he was not involved in scandals.

The Ministry of Saint John the Baptist

John 1:29-34

The Navarre Bible notes are instructive.
"In calling Jesus the 'lamb of God' John
Alludes to Christ's redemptive sacrifice."
John knew the divinity of Jesus.

John the Baptist was born before Jesus.
From Saint Greg, we know that Jesus "is born
Of his mother in time, he was gener-
ated by his Father outside of time."

John bore witness at the Baptism of
Jesus. The mystery of the Blessed
Trinity was revealed. "The dove is the
Symbol of the Holy Spirit." Amen.

John and Jesus were extraordinary
Cousins. They helped us obtain salvation.

Jesus Encounters His First Followers

John 1:35-42

John the Baptist pointed his disciples
To Christ and said, "Behold, the Lamb of God."
The disciples did not want detention.
So they were quickly quite obedient.

Christ turned and asked, "What are you looking for?"
Apostle John asked, "Where are you staying?"
Jesus said to them, "Come, and you will see."
It was a divine, human dialogue.

After Andrew had spent time with Jesus,
Andrew went and found his brother Simon.
Andrew said, "We have found the Messiah."
Then Andrew brought Simon to Jesus Christ.

Jesus Christ changed Simon's name to Cephas.
Cephas means Peter; he was Christ's vicar.

The Ultimate Good Came from Nazareth

John 1:45-51

If the Apostles had played football,
They would have been a great team.
We don't know much about Bartholomew,
So he would have been a lineman.
Let's put him at left guard with the nickname Bart.

Philip found Bartholomew-Nathanael.
We don't know much about Philip either,
So he would have been a lineman too.
Let's put him at left tackle with the nickname Phil.

Since Bart said that Jesus was the Son of God,
Jesus said that Bart "will see heaven opened
And the angels of God ascending and
Descending on the Son of Man."
That would be a great postgame show.

From a Den of Thieves to a House of Prayer

John 2:13-22

When Jesus saw animals and money-
changers in the temple area, He
Was upset. So He cleared them out of there.
Once again the area had clean air.

Jesus could raise the temple in three days.
He was told that it took forty-six years.
Jesus said His body was a temple.
The disciples understood later on.

This passage is sometimes wrongly used to
Justify a loss of temper. Here is
One of my father's impersonations
Of me. "What do you mean I have a bad
Temper? I haven't hit anyone since
Nineteen seventy-five." I rest his case.

The Curing of a Royal Official's Son

John 4:46-54

A royal official traveled twenty
Miles from Capernaum to Cana to ask
Jesus to cure his son who was near death.
The official was humbly persistent.

The official wanted Jesus to go
To Capernaum. Jesus cured long distance.
Miracles call us to faith and belief.
They show God's mercy and mighty power.

When I was a high school junior, I rode
My bike twenty-five miles from Des Plaines to
Wheaton to see someone. She wasn't home.

My hair was brown, curly, and thick. Now my
Hair is white, straight, and thin. God is protec-
ting my marriage. I was too good looking.

Patrick McCaskey

The Miracle of the Loaves and Fishes

John 6:1-15

From the "Workbook for Lectors," we know that
A large crowd had seen Jesus help the sick.
He climbed a mountain with His disciples.
The crowd followed them with a great hunger.

Jesus asked Philip "how can we feed them?"
Philip did the accounting in despair.
Andrew told Christ about a boy with food.
Jesus had five thousand sit on the grass.

Christ multiplied five loaves and two fishes.
They had an excellent sufficiency.
Let this Gospel be a reminder. God
Performs miracles for people of faith.

When I was a child, the bread order for
My family was sixteen loaves a week.

Jesus Discoursed about the Bread of Life

John 6:22-29

After Jesus had multiplied loaves and
Fishes and walked on water, people looked
For Him. They had had an excellent suf-
fiency. So they wanted to thank Him.

Filled with food, they took boat rides to Christ.
This prefigured the altar calls at the
Billy Graham Crusades. "The busses will wait."
Jesus gave us faith and eternal life.

Jesus said to them, "Do not work for food
That perishes but for food that endures
For eternal life." We have Communion.
Catholics can have Communion every day.

Passover has become the Eucharist.
Instead of manna we have Communion.

Christ Is the One Who Reveals the Father

John 6:37-40

Jesus Christ is our gateway to heaven.
He gives us our noble aspirations.

When I was a student at Saint Mary's
In Des Plaines, the City of Destiny,
We had Mass on First Fridays. After Mass,
We consumed sweet rolls and hot chocolate
For ten cents that went to the missions.

When I was a child, at the end of grace
Before meals, my father used to say, "Dear
Lord, please convert the Russians. Our Lady
Help of the sick pray for them. May the souls
Of the faithful departed, through the mer-
cy of God, rest in peace, Amen." Later,
He said, "In your prayers, remember the Bears."

Ark of the Covenant

The Bread of Life Revealed the Father

John 6:44-51

God spoke through Isaiah and Jeremiah
About the covenant with His people.
When the Messiah comes, it will be sealed.
God will write it on people's hearts with blood.

Christ used the images of food and drink.
Noble aspirations are satisfied.

Jesus is present in the Eucharist.
The Eucharist is central to the Church.
It's in John Paul II's last encyclical.
As we say in sports, you could look it up.

Jesus Christ is the Word of God made flesh.
He's not a baseball player like Tom Tresh.
Jesus Christ has great credibility.
He spoke with ultimate authority.

The Bread of Life Is in the Eucharist

John 6:51-58

From the Lectors Workbook, we know that "John
The Evangelist is instructing us
About the value of the Eucharist.
It is offered...from the altar as bread and wine
Transformed into the" Lamb's Body and Blood.

From the Navarre Bible commentary,
We know that "Jesus...is inviting us
To partake often of His Body, as
Nourishment for our souls," our daily bread.

Transubstantiation is wonderful.
We can eat and drink the Lamb's Flesh and Blood.
The Church is a halfway house to heaven.

Since exhumation is part of canon-
ization, I do not want cremation.

Patrick McCaskey

Jesus Went from God to Jerusalem

John 7:1-2, 10, 25-30

Those who accept Christ are His family.
Some people do not see Christ as Savior.
Jesus has power to bring salvation.
Listen to His words; they are obvious.

Christ waited for the right time to be born.
He allowed Himself to be put to death.
Let us acknowledge Him for what He did.
This requires conversion of heart and mind.

The Navarre Bible notes are instructive.
To understand and appreciate Christ
Let us strive and thrive to be like Jesus.
What would Christ do is good for me and you.

Every day is Christmas; each day is Lent.
Preparing for heaven is time well spent.

The Writing of Jesus Christ in the Dirt

John 8:1-11

Early in the morning, Jesus Christ was
In the temple area. When people
Came to Jesus, He sat down and taught them.

A woman was caught in adultery.
She was brought to Jesus for a ruling.
Jesus wrote something unknown in the dirt.

He invited the sinless to stone her.
No one was qualified, except Jesus.
Jesus told her not to sin anymore.

Seamus Heaney compared the writing of
Jesus Christ in the dirt to poetry.

Poetry, like the dirt writing, marks time.
"Poetry holds attention for a space."
Poetry functions as concentration.

Patrick McCaskey

Isaac Was Restored, Jesus Christ Arose

John 8:51-59

God told Abraham he would have a son.
After Isaac's birth, the work was not done.
God told Abraham: sacrifice Isaac.
Abraham agreed; he did not look back.

Right after the test, Isaac was restored.
When you work with God, you are never bored.
Abraham Isaac are quite a story.
They were righteous and worked for God's glory.

Christ died for our sins; He was quite the Man.
He arose from the dead: what a great plan.
After our earthly death, live forever.
We can live with God, leaving Him never.

Christ died for our sins, including fumbles.
With God in Heaven, no one there mumbles.

Jesus Cured a Man Who Had Been Born Blind

John 9:1-41

Jesus spat on the ground and made spittle.
Then He anointed the man's eyes with clay.
Christ said, "Go, wash in the pool of Siloam"
"So he went and washed and came back seeing."

Jesus Christ gave light to the blind man's eyes.
Christ also enlightened the blind man's mind.
The blind man believed in Jesus as Christ.
We also have that opportunity.

This miracle is like our Baptism.
Our soul is cleansed. We have the light of faith.

I had eye problems thirty-seven years.
From "The Quiet Man," "Those were the bad days."
Doctor Rubenstein restored my vision
Through two successful corneal transplants.

Jesus Christ Is the Gateway to Heaven

John 10:1-10

David was a shepherd who became a king.
Christ was a king who became a shepherd.
Jesus fulfilled the ancient prophecies
Of Jeremiah and Ezekiel.

The illustration of Jesus as the
Good Shepherd shows God's love for each of us.
Like the Waltons at bedtime, He calls all
Of us: "Good night Saint Mary's; follow Me."

Jesus speaks through the Church; let us listen
To the priests, the cardinals, and the pope.
If they say something that we do not like
Let's not mope. It's the feast day of Saint George.

Saint George slayed dragons and rescued maidens.
Let's be chivalrous and charitable.

Jesus Christ Laid Down His Life for His Sheep

John 10:11-18

The Church is a flock with human shepherds.
Jesus leads us and brings us to pasture.
He knows us and calls each of us by name.
We have birth names and Confirmation names.

Priests take care of their flocks willingly. They
Are wonderful examples for their flocks.
They want salvation for every human.
They provide us with Holy Communion.

When we are in trouble, they do not run.
There are times when they let us have some fun.
They do not want anyone to be lost.
Like Saint Ignatius, they don't count the cost.

Jesus Christ gave His life for everyone.
Jesus Christ is a Hall of Fame shepherd.

The Attempt to Stone Jesus Was Postponed

John 10:31-42

Jesus and the Father are unified.
Divine Revelation is quite a guide.
Christ became human to sanctify man.
Salvation is a most wonderful plan.

To avoid getting stoned Jesus withdrew.
You can follow Christ. Won't you come too?
The Navarre Bible notes are instructive.
They help us to cope with the destructive.

John the Baptist prepared us for Jesus.
Followers of John drew near to Jesus.
John said that Jesus is the Messiah.
Christ quoted Scripture and did miracles.

Work in the name of God is not wasted.
The fruit of Christians is always tasted.

Christ Reacts to the Death of Lazarus

John 11:1-45

Lazarus was ill. Martha and Mary
Sent for Jesus. Jesus waited two days.
Lazarus died. Jesus walked two miles from
Jerusalem to Bethany. Christ wept.
The Navarre Bible notes are instructive.
"This is the shortest verse in the Bible."

Jesus raised Lazarus from the dead.
Jesus showed power over death. This is
A sign of our future resurrection.

Saint Augustine saw risen Lazarus
As everyone's reconciliation.
Lazarus came out of the tomb still bound.
We go to confession still guilty.
Lazarus became loosed. We're forgiven.

Christ Announces His Glorification

John 12:20-33

From the Navarre Bible commentary,
We know that "Jesus...is...a seed that" dies
"And thereby produces abundant fruit."
He was humbled; then He was glorified.

Every suffering and contradiction
Shares Christ's cross. We're redeemed and exalted.
When we die to ourselves without a thought
To our own comfort or desires and plans,
We're supernaturally effective.

Christ fell three times on the walk to His death.
I threw three interceptions in one game.
Jesus rose from the dead to His glory.
I made Catholic All-American.

Jesus the Son Reveals God the Father

John 14:1-6

Jesus predicted Peter's denial.
That seemed to have depressed the Apostles.
Jesus wanted them to be joyful. So
He told them, "that He is going away
To prepare a place for them in heaven"
Despite shortcomings, failures, and setbacks.

The quotes are from the Navarre Bible notes.

Jesus "is Life because from all eter-
nity he shares in divine life with the
Father...through grace" we can have divine life.

Christ spoke in iambic pentameter:
Poetry, ten syllables in each line.

"I am the way and the truth and the life.
No one comes to the Father, but by me."

Intimate Conversation with Jesus

John 14:15-21

The Ten Commandments are not suggestions.
God showed the way. Let there be no questions.
We keep the Commandments; Jesus is loved.
The Commandments are kept; Satan is shoved.

With the Advocate, there are no small ways.
The Advocate will be with us always.
The public life of Jesus was three years.
When we're obedient, we hear His cheers.

Jesus is in the Father; He's in us.
We're all working together; so don't fuss.
Let's observe the Commandments all the time.
Love God always; that's our mountain to climb.

We love Jesus; we're loved by His Father.
The Spirit tells Satan not to bother.

The Advocate Teaches Us Everything

John 14:21-26

From the Navarre Bible commentary,
We know that Jesus wants us to show our
Love for God through "generous and faithful
Self-giving" and obeying the Commandments.

Jesus is our Advocate in Heaven.
The Spirit is our Advocate on earth.
When we're disheartened, the Spirit lifts us.
Spirit give us a preview of Heaven.

Saint Paul said that "each of us is a temple
Of the Holy Spirit. The Trinity
Dwells in the soul of each person." Spirit
Helps us understand what Jesus Christ said.

Today is the feast day of Saint Pius V.
He was known for his strict fasting and prayer.

Patrick McCaskey

Jesus is the Vine, We are the Branches

John 15:1-8

The night before Jesus died, He spoke well.
He is the vine; His Father grows the vine.
We receive tribulations and temptations.
They make us stronger; we serve God longer.

My earthly father once said to me, "It's
Up to you but you're doing it all wrong."
Accountability, encouragement
Help us get pruned of our ungodliness.

When we are with Jesus Christ, we sin less,
We do holy works, and we help others.
Mass the sacraments, Bible study,
And daily devotions keep us attuned.

The Holy Trinity helps us stay pruned.
When Christ is our vine, we are mighty fine.

The Father Loved Jesus, Jesus Loves Us

John 15:9-17

Brotherly love led Jesus to the cross.
Jesus proved His love for us on the cross.
Love inspires us to keep the Commandments.
Love for Christ leads us to obedience.

From the Navarre Bible commentary,
We know that Jesus Christ is our best friend.

After Christ had ascended to heaven,
Matthias became the twelfth Apostle.

From the book called, "Who's Who in the Bible,"
We know that "There had to be twelve to cor-
Respond to the twelve tribes of Israel."

If the Apostles had played football, they
Would have been a great team. Matthias, who
Replaced Judas, would have been the kicker.

The Holy Spirit Testifies to Christ

John 15:26-16:4

Christ revealed Himself through His miracles.
We accept Him; our sins are forgiven.

Jesus sends The Holy Spirit who testifies.
The Spirit helps us understand Jesus.
Our hearts are opened; we don't "fall away."

Father created a wonderful world.
Christ died for our sins, including fumbles.
Holy Spirit is always there for us.

God the Father allowed His Son to die.
Jesus ascended and sent The Spirit.
The Holy Spirit consoles and comforts.
Trials have good purpose; let our faith be seen.
The Trinity has cooperation.
They don't misbehave like the three stooges.

Poems About the Gospel

United in Prayer

Unbroken Succession Through The Spirit

John 16:12-15

Jesus Christ revealed the truth. The Holy
Spirit helped the Apostles understand.
The Apostles were lost until Pentecost.
The Paraclete provides love to the Church.

The three divine Persons are equal.
Remember Saint Patrick and the shamrock.
Father Hesburgh was in many meetings.
Before each he prayed, "Come Holy Spirit."

When we ask for the Spirit, He is there.
He is even there when we do not ask.
Persecutions and trials don't dishearten.
Let's turn difficulties to good purpose.

Do you know three people who are a cross
Between The Trinity and the three stooges?

Poems About the Gospel

Jesus Prayed for the Apostles and Us

John 17:11b-19

Jesus Christ asked His Father to keep His
Apostles in His name for communion
With Him. Their unity would reflect the
Unity of the Blessed Trinity.

The Trinity reigns with mutual love
And self-giving. We can discover our
True selves only when we give ourselves.

Jesus invites us to receive God's love.
Be in the world without being worldly.
Jesus died for us and gave us true life.

Jesus prayed this at the Last Supper.
Knute Rockne said, "Win one for the Gipper."

Patrick McCaskey

Jesus Christ Wrote More than the Our Father

John 17:20-26

Christ taught us to pray with the Our Father.
In this passage, He teaches us again.
When we have struggles, let's depend on Christ.
We can suffer with confidence in Him.

Perhaps your suffering is poetry.
This poem will be over in a minute.

Thank you for listening. This is better
Than talking to myself. It's great to be
With you. Let us be Hall of Fame Legates.

From Scott Hahn, we know that family is
The first society. Like Pope Francis,
Let us celebrate the good of the Church.

154

The Passion and the Death of Jesus Christ

John 18:1-19:42

Those who arrested Jesus were in awe.
We should do God's will the way Jesus did.
Isaac and Jesus were obedient.
Before the chief priests, Jesus was transparent.

Jesus Christ forgave Peter's denials
Because Peter had a great repentance.
Jesus was grateful for John's faithfulness.
Thank God for the Sacrament of Penance.

When Jesus was before Pilate, Christ did
Not say much. He was like Gary Cooper.
Jesus Christ was whipped and then crowned with
thorns.
Then Pilate handed Christ over for death.

Jesus carried His cross to Calvary.
His side was pierced and His cup was finished.

Patrick McCaskey

Dialogue between Pilate and Jesus

John 18:33b-37

Jesus had a spiritual mission.
He did not seek independence from Rome.
This was hard for Pilate to understand.

Christ's Kingdom prepares us for Judgement Day.
From the "Roman Missal," Preface of the
Mass of Christ the King, we know that the King-
dom of Jesus really is truth and life;
Holiness and grace; justice, love, and peace.

From the "Workbook for Lectors," we know that
"The humble service and total sacri-
fice of Christ the King is the truth that res-
cues humanity from itself and re-
stores the dignity of the human race."

Jesus Christ did not need Perry Mason.

Jesus on the Cross Gave Us His Mother

John 19:25-27

When we call out signals and our voice cracks,
When we dribble down court and punt the ball,
When we're late for practice because of JUG,
Let us remember, we have God's Mother.

When we lose a close game to a rival,
When we are not heard at a pep rally,
When we are cut from the sophomore team,
Let us remember, we have God's Mother.

When we don't pass the football physical,
When we nearly drown at swimming practice,
When we run track like a football player,
Let us remember, we have God's Mother.

When we make All-Area quarterback,
Let us remember, to thank God's Mother.

Patrick McCaskey

The Empty Tomb Fulfilled
the Prophecies

John 20:1-9

Mary Magdalene was first at the Tomb.
When Peter and John arrived at the Tomb,
John let Peter enter first because he
Was the elder. John had run faster; Peter
Might have told John to do some stretching.

From the Navarre Bible commentary,
We know that "the empty tomb, the linen
Cloths, the napkin in a place by itself"
Were the evidence that Jesus arose.
Detective Columbo was not needed.

John saw and believed and Peter achieved.
Peter and John did not understand the
Scripture. They needed Bible Study.
Let's go therefore and do likewise. Amen.

Poems About the Gospel

My Lord and My God

Patrick McCaskey

Jesus Appeared to the Apostles Twice

John 20:19-31

Christ gave the Apostles a commission.
He started the Sacrament of Penance.
When Jesus appeared to the Apostles
For the first time, Thomas was marked absent.

Tom doubted what the Apostles told him.
He would even have questioned a football coach.
When Jesus appeared to the Apostles
Again, Thomas became a believer.

Navarre Bible notes sum up John's purpose,
"To have people believe that Jesus is
The Christ, the Messiah announced by the
Old Testament prophets (and) the son of God."

This passage has two great quotes. Christ said, "Peace
Be with you." Tom said, "My Lord and my God."

The Catch of One Hundred Fifty-Three Fish

John 21:1-14

John loved Jesus Christ and recognized Him.
Peter got to Christ before the others.
When Jesus ate with them, He proved Himself.
Jesus was not a ghost; He had risen.

Saint Paul wrote, "Love is patient. Love is kind."
Saint Josemaria wrote "Love, love is
Farsighted. Love is the first to appre-
ciate kindness." Sir Paul McCartney wrote
And sang, "Love doesn't come in a minute."

From the Navarre Bible notes, we know that,
"The boat is the Church, whose unity is
Symbolized by the net that does not tear;
The sea is the world; Peter in the boat
Stands for supreme authority in the Church."

Patrick McCaskey

After Breakfast, Jesus Asked Three Questions

John 21:15-19

The disciples had fasted all night.
Their stomachs were probably very light.
Jesus helped them break their fast with breakfast.
Fried fishes were a wonderful repast.

Jesus asked Peter a question three times.
Peter replied to Jesus without chimes.
The mandate from Jesus was very clear.
Love and build the Church and be of good cheer.

Christ said to Peter who was not asleep,
"Feed my lambs, tend my sheep, and feed my sheep."
When Peter was young, he went anywhere.
When he was mature, he was Fred Astaire.

Jesus showed Peter choreography.
Jesus had said to Peter, "Follow Me."

Photo Credits

All photographs are reproduced with permission.

Page	Photo Description	Source
Cover	Angelicum Cloister, Pontifical University of St Thomas Aquinas https://www.flickr.com/photos/paullew/27078124291/in/photostream/	Fr. Lawrence Lew, O.P.
IX	Christ in Majesty with Evangelists, mosaic on the chancel arch at Westminster Cathedral, https://www.flickr.com/photos/paullew/2951294076/in/album-72157625338936185/	Fr. Lawrence Lew, O.P.
5	Christ our Peace, Mosaic of Christ symbolized in the Abbey of the Dormition, on Mount Sion in Jerusalem. https://www.flickr.com/photos/paullew/48178377451/	Fr. Lawrence Lew, O.P.
25	Stargazer, Bethany Retreat House in Dickson County, Tennessee, Nashville Dominican Sisters, https://www.flickr.com/photos/paullew/28846739105/in/album-72157594551019946/	Fr. Lawrence Lew, O.P.

Patrick McCaskey

Page	Photo Description	Source
30	Papal Keyes, Stone carving from the facade of the Cathedral of Rome, St John Lateran., https://www.flickr.com/photos/paullew/49568745707/	Fr. Lawrence Lew, O.P.
43	Herald of the Messiah, Statue entitled 'The Young Saint John the Baptist' by Giovanni Francesco Susini, National Gallery of Art, Washington DC., https://www.flickr.com/photos/paullew/27771626622/in/photostream/	Fr. Lawrence Lew, O.P.
54	Light on the Rotunda, Shafts of light from the dome of the Rotunda of the building that surrounds the Empty Tomb of Jesus Christ, https://www.flickr.com/photos/paullew/47064388624/	Fr. Lawrence Lew, O.P.
74	Visitation, Luca della Robbia's sublime 'The Visitation', dating from about 1445, from the church of San Giovanni Fuorcivitas in Pistoia, https://www.flickr.com/photos/paullew/41747215414/	Fr. Lawrence Lew, O.P.
83	Dominican friar prays in Blackfriars church, Oxford. https://www.flickr.com/photos/paullew/2852672177/in/album-72157594386960467/	Fr. Lawrence Lew, O.P.
92	Saint Paul Statue from Sainte Chapelle in Paris, https://www.flickr.com/photos/paullew/46145841954/.	Fr. Lawrence Lew, O.P.

Poems About the Gospel

Page	Photo Description	Source
110	Saint Margaret of Scotland, stained glass by Webb is from St Mungo's Cathedral in Glasgow. https://www.flickr.com/photos/paullew/8190519340/in/album-72157629979810390/	Fr. Lawrence Lew, O.P.
133	Stained glass window from Holy Rosary Priory church in Portland, OR., https://www.flickr.com/photos/paullew/50232179427/	Fr. Lawrence Lew, O.P.
151	United in Prayer, Pentecost, Detail from an altarpiece in San Francisco's Catholic Cathedral., https://www.flickr.com/photos/paullew/49929337846/	Fr. Lawrence Lew, O.P.
159	My Lord and My God, Relief sculpture from the chapel of the Nashville Dominican Sister's retreat house, Bethany. https://www.flickr.com/photos/paullew/50070765558/	Fr. Lawrence Lew, O.P.

Patrick McCaskey

Patrick McCaskey was born at Saint Francis Hospital in Evanston. He played basketball and baseball for Saint Mary's School in Des Plaines. He played football and ran track for Notre Dame High School in Niles. He ran cross-country and track for Cheshire Academy in Connecticut. Pat's mom and dad had 11 children: 3 girls and 8 boys. His parents encouraged faith, hard work, reading, and a good laugh.

Pat was a contributing editor to the literary magazines at Loyola University in Chicago and Indiana University. He started working for the Chicago Bears in 1974. He went to DePaul University at night during the off-seasons and earned a master's degree.

Pat is a Chicago Bears' Board Member and a Bears' Vice President. He is the Chairman of Sports Faith International which recognizes people who are successful in sports while leading exemplary lives. Sports Faith has a radio station, WSFI, 88.5 FM, which broadcasts in northern Illinois and southern Wisconsin.

Pat is the author of many books including:
Bear with Me: A Family History of George Halas and the Chicago Bears;
Sports and Faith: Stories of the Devoted and the Devout;
Pillars of the NFL: Coaches Who Have Won Three or More Championships;
Sports and Faith: More Stories of the Devoted and the Devout;
Pilgrimage;
Worthwhile Struggle;
Sportsmanship;
Papa Bear and the Chicago Bears' Winning Ways; and
Poems About the Gospel

Pat and his wife, Gretchen, have three sons: Ed, Tom, and Jim; two daughters in law: Elizabeth and Emily; four granddaughters: Grace, Charlotte, Violet Min, and Madeline; and a grandson, Pat.